Wishing you many happy "peaceful" gardening hours. See page 45!

OLD WIVES' LORE
FOR GARDENERS

Old Wives' Lore for Gardeners

MAUREEN
& BRIDGET
BOLAND

THE BODLEY HEAD
LONDON SYDNEY
TORONTO

© Maureen and Bridget Boland 1976
ISBN 0 370 11369 1
Printed and bound in Great Britain for
The Bodley Head Ltd
9 Bow Street, London WC2E 7AL
by W & J Mackay Ltd, Chatham
Set in Monotype Ehrhardt
First published 1976
Sixth impression 1977

The decorations have been chosen from a number of sources, including Thomas Bewick (b. 1753) and his school (e.g. pages 41 and 57) and Gerard's *Herball*, first published in 1597 (pages 9, 10, 21, 25, 33, 34, 48, 51 and 62).

CONTENTS

FOREWORD

We are not Old Wives ourselves, being in fact old spinsters; nor are we professional gardeners in any sense. We collected the tips in this book because we needed them. Our garden for some forty years had been at the basement level of our house in Pimlico. It was pitch dark, and the soil was the heavy clay of the reclaimed marshland once belonging to Westminster Abbey half a mile away. Gerard in his Herbal speaks of water lilies growing there, and a very old botanist whom we knew as children used to talk of gathering rare marsh flowers as a boy on the site of our house. We learned by trial and a great deal of error what could be grown there, and from studying books that recommended plants that would flourish in damp shade. So many of these were poisonous that we once contemplated going into business as market gardeners to supply would-be murderers who hesitated to sign chemists' registers for their needs. We then lived for a few years in South Kensington, where we laboured with more success at street level in a back garden twenty feet by twenty, which we opened by request to the public in aid of the District Nurses Fund, and which was much admired. It was even photographed for two books and several magazines—but really only because we had placed arch-shaped full-length mirrors in the back wall, giving the idea of two gardens for the price of one to many Londoners.

We then moved to our present house in Hampshire, working a garden in recently-cleared woodland on a light sandy soil on a steep hillside facing due south in a little suntrap of a valley, where the little learning we had acquired by gardening on Thames mud mostly in the dark was a dead loss. Needing to learn fast, we pestered everyone we met in the district for advice on what grew well locally and how to care for it; and we found that we were beginning to amass a store of curious information. We began to ask all our friends, wherever they lived, for the sort of lore their grandmothers had passed down to them. Modern scientific gardening books we read, of course; but we found in old books too so much practical advice of the grandmotherly kind that the new books never covered that we decided to pass it all on to those who are not afraid of finding a certain amount of superstition mingled with good sense.

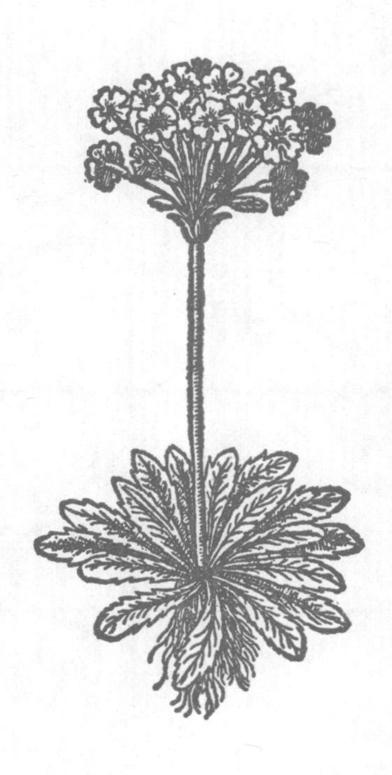

PLANTING

Consider the Moon

Every Old Wife will tell you to sow seed and to transplant only with a waxing, never a waning moon. The scientists have now caught up with this, discovering the effects of lunar rhythms on the earth's magnetic field which in turn affect growth. They have established that all water everywhere, including that inside the tiniest living organism, moves in tides like the sea. The moon also affects the earth's atmosphere so that statistically it is more likely to rain heavily (just as you would like immediately after planting) immediately after a full or a new moon. They say that a potato grown at constant levels of heat and light under laboratory conditions will still show a growth rhythm that reflects the lunar pattern. The Old Wife, without laboratory conditions or statistical tables, learned from experience how best to get her plants off to a good start.

Sow seed generously

One for the rook, one for the crow,
One to die and one to grow.

Sartorial

It is curious how often in old herbals we are advised to sow not only when the moon is full but naked, ourselves, at the time. 'The best husbandmen,' writes one, 'would have the seedsman of turnips or rapes to be naked when he sows them, and in sowing to protest that this which he doth is for himself and his neighbours.' Presumably, it was hoped that the gods might look more kindly on the naked, innocent amateur than on the prosperous market gardener. Perhaps, though, the advice was not always given for purely magical reasons: we should not sow when the ground is too cold for the good of the seed, and are less likely to do so if we are told we must be naked when we do it. We have heard that in Lincolnshire, to test whether the soil was in the right condition for sowing barley, farmers used to take off their trousers and sit on the ground: if it was comfortable for them it would be comfortable for the barley. With the greater density of population, the modern gardener will probably be content to test the soil with a bared elbow, as a mother does the water for her baby's bath.

Mattresses for Beans

It was not actually an Old Wife who told us to put hair in the bottom of a trench when planting beans, but a hairdresser who abandoned his salon to go round the countryside doing the hair of invalids and elderly pensioners in their own homes. His only regret for his salon is that nowadays, working alone, he can collect less hair.

Country buses are excellent places for meeting Old Wives, and when one of us passed this tip on to her neighbour on one she said that her grandmother used to tease out old horsehair mattresses for this purpose, and also to use the results of grooming her dog and cats, as well as herself and her children. Noxious little creatures in the soil, she said, would become entangled in it, and the horsehair was strong and sharp enough to prick them to death. Anyone who as a child with bare legs has sat on a horsehair sofa can well believe this; but scientists have also now discovered that hair is full of valuable mineral and chemical properties, supplying trace elements not otherwise easily available.

Sowing Beans

Candlemas Day stick beans in the clay,
Throw candle and candlestick right away.

The second part of this admonition may not have been magical so much as economical in intent: the thrifty Old Wife perhaps considered that by 2nd February one should not need candle-light to get up by, dinner would have been eaten at three o'clock, the evening stew, already prepared, could be eaten by firelight, and one should go to bed early and certainly not read in bed.

Roll seeds of beans and peas in paraffin to deter mice.

Planting Herbs

Never plant the same kind of herb in the same place twice in succession, said an eighteenth-century herbalist, replacing a 'hot' herb with a 'cool' one—a sound rule-of-thumb for rotation that will prevent exhausting the soil of the particular properties one plant or the other needs.

Planting Cabbages

Twist a spiral of narrow tinfoil round the roots of a young cabbage plant to inhibit the larvae of the cabbage fly.

On the surface lay a piece of creosoted string or a narrow ring of creosoted felt four inches away round the plant to repel attack.

Planting Carrots

Crumble mothballs and mix them with the soil against the larvae of carrot fly. This has proved a sovereign remedy where the fly is otherwise rife.

Laying a length of tarred or creosoted string on the surface between the rows two inches from the plants has also been recommended if the former precaution has been neglected.

Planting Mint

The mixing of bonfire ash with the soil, often recommended when planting other herbs, can be fatal to mint, and should not be used even as a mulch.

Planting Garlic

The savour of young garlic, an old herbalist says, will be sweeter (whatever that may mean) if you crush the cloves a little before planting to bruise them, and also if you set olive stones among them.

Dripping for Roses

Our own most valuable, original discovery as Old Wives was made, as surely most must have been, by mistake. The over-enthusiastic use of detergents when they first became available caused the grease in washing-up water, suspended in the bubbles, to form gradually a thick cake of fat under the manhole cover outside the kitchen window. We lifted it out, but this was in London when food rationing was still in force after the War, when the throwing in the dustbin of what looked like a mass of edible dripping, eighteen inches by twelve and at least two inches thick, was unthinkable. We buried it darkly at dead of night in the back garden—not far, as it chanced, from the roots of a climbing rose which had never done very well. That year the rose flowered stunningly, and it flourished ever after. We never planted a rose again without burying fat below it, begging extra from the surprised butcher.

When we moved to the country we continued, the first year, the same practice. Every single one of our beautiful new roses was instantly dug up by the foxes that abound in the neighbouring woods, and we have had to desist. For townsfolk, however, or those with walled gardens, it cannot be too highly recommended.

We once read of a family in France who were said to bury the unwanted babies of maidens of the villagery under their vines, presumably on the same principle, but let it not be said that we actually advocate this.

Planting Strawberries

For strawberries, and only for strawberries, incorporate scrapings of topsoil from below pines and spruces when planting, and thereafter mulch with pine and spruce needles, crushed fircones and even twigs; this is said to improve the flavour.

If there are such trees near the house, you will find that needles lodge among tiles and are washed down into the gutters. The labour of clearing them is rewarded if there is a use (apart from the merely negative one of unblocked drainpipes) for the product.

Transplanting out of season

When for some reason it is necessary to transplant at a time of year when it is really too cold, puddle the plants in using hot water instead of cold. This, surprisingly, really does not damage the roots.

Bracken for Fuchsias

In the light soil of our warm and sheltered little valley we leave even tender fuchsias outdoors all the winter, so far without disaster, but we always cover them with mounds of bracken against the frosts. An Old Wife seeing this one autumn was shocked. She said that there was nothing better to dig in under fuchsias when planting them than chopped green bracken, which would encourage the roots to go down; but that they had such a passion for it that they would tend towards the surface if bracken was laid there, suffering accordingly in a hot, dry season. We now compromise, supplying bracken to both ends.

LIKES

In so unscientific a work as this, we hesitate to use the word symbiosis, which is the one that serious people now employ when writing of plants that get on well together. Older gardeners found out by trial and error what grew well in proximity and what did not without realising that they were using the Bio-Dynamic Method, happily ignorant of the nature of root excretions and the activity of organic compounds. Now that such knowledge is available, and in a form digestible by the unscientifically minded as well as by experts, no one should plan the layout of flower or kitchen garden without references to a little handbook called *Companion Plants*, by Helen Philbrick and Richard B. Gregg (published by Watkins). Only the laws of copyright prevent us copying out large sections from it, and we have had reluctantly to limit ourselves here to such information as we have gleaned for ourselves elsewhere.

Marigolds with everything

When we were children, we spent every summer in a little house in a fishing village in northern France, which we rented from M and

Mme Noël. They lived there all the year round, retreating to a corner of the house when we arrived but continuing to keep up the garden, the only one in the village. They grew vegetables only for the house, but they sold the flowers. There was a bell that jangled when anyone came through the door in the high garden wall, and shy young men used to put a cautious hand up to clutch it as they slipped in, lest the horrible little Bolands, lying in wait, should gossip all round the village that they were courting. On the feasts of saints that were the name-days of the most popular girls, half-stifled clatterings of the bell could be heard at intervals all day long. The

village was built on pure sea sand, but inside our little walled garden the soil was as rich as chocolate. Everything grew. M Noël's particular pride were the dahlias that he bred, as big as soup plates, planted near the outside privy. It was not a beautiful garden, for flowers of each kind grew rigidly in commercially practical rows, and there were for our taste far too many of the 'everlasting' flowers in great demand for taking to the cemetery; but nowhere, surely, were plants ever so healthy or blooms so big. We learned the French names of flowers before we knew the English ones, and were much surprised when we found that what we knew as Indian Buttonholes were called in England French marigolds, but then supposed that it was because the French, as witness M Noël, had such an insensate passion for them. Every bed in the garden was edged with a miniature hedge of them, and the large beds had rows of them down the middle as well. Asked, since the scent was not attractive, why he grew so many of them, M Noël replied: 'They're good for everything.' Since he also grew many plants out of which Mme Noël made the loathsome tisanes she would try to make anyone drink who was ill, we supposed the marigolds were specifics against all the evils that the flesh is heir to; but in fact the health he was concerned with was that of his plants. Both the aroma and the excretions from the roots are invaluable, whether in flower or vegetable garden or in the greenhouse. We have since seen them often as edging plants in cottage gardens in England, and do not suppose that the cottagers, any more than M Noël, were aware that what they did was to kill nematodes in the soil, as well as whitefly. Potatoes and tomatoes need them badly.

Tagetes minuta is even more potent than the French (*Tagetes patula*) or the African marigold; and there must have been wise Old Wives in ancient Mexico, where it was sacred to the goddess of agriculture.

Nettles within reason

Nettles can hardly be allowed to rampage all over the garden, but in fact they stimulate the growth of all plants in their neighbourhood while actually growing, as well as being the best thing in the world to hasten the decomposing of a compost heap while providing it with rich ingredients. In the kitchen garden it is advised to grow controlled clumps of them, particularly between currant bushes, which will thereby fruit better and be more resistant to disease; and nothing is better when taking in a new area for any soft fruit than to use an old nettle-bed that has enriched its own soil for many years with its own compost. It is a great relief to the overworked gardener, when someone spots a nettle that in fact is not meant to be there, to be able to say, in mummerset dialect, 'Ee, now, dinna thee move thon, thon be excreting nitrogen, silica, iron, protein, phosphates, formic acid and other mineral salts, thon be.'

Doctor Foxglove

Where old cottage gardens still survive, plants that over many years have been found to grow well together will be seen still doing so in what to the suburban-trained eye will seem a terrible muddle. When carriage lamps appear on either side of the cottage door and one of those gardens fit for the ideal home is laid out, among the first things to go on the bonfire (not even the compost heap) are the ordinary old purple foxgloves with which the whole place will have been dotted. Yet the cottager's old wife could have told the newcomers there is nothing to stimulate growth and help disease resistance like the common foxglove. Apart from keeping plants healthier, they will improve the storage qualities of such things as potatoes, tomatoes and apples grown near them.

Doctor Camomile

Old gardeners used to use camomile like a visiting physician: planted beside a delicate or ailing plant for a short while it would improve its health immensely, and such herbs as mint would develop far more savour. But after a while (in fact when the clump of camomile grew too large), as though the patient had become over-dependent on the doctor and tiresomely hypochondriac, it would weaken again. The solution was to remove the camomile when it had done its work, leaving improved soil behind it in the vicinity of the plant that had been strengthened, only to replace it with a new young plant a good while later if necessary. The 'sweet breath thereof', or, as the scientists would say, the exhalation from the leaves, was considered as beneficial to neighbouring plants as it was pleasant to humans when trodden underfoot, so that camomile paths in herb gardens were particularly recommended; but this would seem to contradict the warning that not too much of it should be grown for too long in the vicinity of some plants. It is held to be entirely good for cabbages in any quantity and, if planted a yard or so apart, for onions.

Herbs outside the herb garden

Apart from the fact that growing pot herbs near the house is practical for the housewife, there is something mediaeval in the idea of a garden of herbs growing all together that appeals to most of us, as though at any time we might surprise there lords and ladies strolling 'richly dight', or a virgin sitting by the sundial or the fountain with a unicorn, its head upon her lap. But if we take the advice of Old Wives we must also grow some of our herbs elsewhere, for the good of other plants. Strawberries are particularly helped by borage, and sage, mint, thyme and rosemary are good for cabbages.

It is lucky that parsley is so decorative, for it encourages bees all over the garden, and in cottage gardens, those models of good sense that look so haphazard, it is often grown as an edging plant alternating with sweet alyssum where the suburban gardener will grow the lobelia. It is particularly valuable grown among roses, where it increases their scent, and (though you will not need it for this purpose if you plant garlic as you should—*see page* 37) it helps to repel greenfly. It is good for tomatoes, and also for asparagus.

Vegetables that make good neighbours

Since lists of which goes well with what make complicated reading (carrots, peas, beans, leeks and turnips all agree well, for instance, but of these only carrots should be planted near onions and garlic), a table would seem the simplest thing to follow. It should be pointed out that in many

	PLANT	HELPFUL	HARMFUL
1	Asparagus	11 W	
2	Beans	4 5 8 10 12 W	7
3	Cabbage family	X Y	7 10 Z
4	Carrots	2 5 6 7 8 12 W	
5	Leeks	2 4 8 12	
6	Lettuce	4 10	
7	Onions, Garlic	4	2 3 10
8	Peas	2 4 5 12 X	7
9	Potatoes	2 10 X	11 Y
10	Strawberries	2 6	3
11	Tomatoes	1 W X	9
12	Turnips	2 4 5 W	
W	Parsley		
X	Marigolds		

Y Rosemary, mint, thyme, camomile Z Rue

cases it is not that A is particularly good for B, but that B is particularly good for A (parsley, for instance, doing more for asparagus than asparagus does for parsley), but this need not concern us when planting them near together. That some things actively dislike each other is perhaps more important than that others do each other good. We have added to the vegetables in the table certain other plants which are helpful or otherwise to them.

Lest you rue the day

Apart from being bad for cabbages, rue is bad for many herbs. Some Old Wives say that it can make sage planted near it positively poisonous; but it is more likely simply to kill it, as it may basil.

Many people plant gladioli in the vegetable garden, simply because the stakes that they need look ugly in the flower beds. They are, however, extremely bad for peas and beans, and so bad for strawberries that these will suffer from them planted up to fifty feet away.

Ash trees

The ash has always been considered to have magical properties. Whatever its virtues for witches and warlocks, honest Old Wives would have you never plant it in the garden. They say that it is so greedy it takes all the good out of the ground for many yards around it.

We have had two curious experiences with it. We had grown a rose for some time up an old tree at the top of a slope, and it was finally brought down by the wind. A good distance down the slope grew a young mountain ash whose upper branches now came high enough for us to arch the rose across the slope to grow through them, making, we hoped, a splendid natural rose arch. Every single branch of the rose died back to exactly the point where it first touched the ash.

On another occasion, short of some pea-sticks from more suitable trees, we used ash. The sweet peas we were trying to grow on them absolutely refused to cling, the tendrils we tried to wind round them uncoiling at once.

Remember, however, if you decide to fell an ash already growing in the garden, that all old country people would warn you to ask its permission first. How it will signify its assent we do not know. Perhaps the civility of asking is all that is required. It makes splendid firewood, and there are several versions of an old rhyme about how long to keep different kinds of wood before burning them, all of which end:

But ash new or ash old
Is fit for a queen with a crown of gold.

Oak and Walnut

'If an oak be set near unto a walnut tree it will not live.' This we have on the authority of a translation of Pliny by Philemon Holland, Doctor of Physicke, 1601, and alas it is not clear from this version whether it is the oak or the walnut that will die. We have not, by some mischance, the Latin by us; but frankly we doubt whether we should achieve any more specific agreement of the pronoun than the good Doctor's.

Laurels

Even if it cannot be said to belong strictly in this section, we cannot resist passing on the information that the growing of one shrub at least is good for people growing in its vicinity. Friar Bartholomew hath it that 'the land that beareth the laurel tree is safe from lightning both in field and house'.

CONTROLLING WEEDS

You need not have Couch Grass

In an area badly infested with couch we sowed turnip seed thickly, as we were advised. We now have no couch. You may not want turnips (and, sown so lavishly, you will not get very large ones anyway), but you certainly don't want couch. We have since heard lupins and tomatoes recommended for the same purpose, but have had no need to try them.

Ground Ivy, Horsetail, Ground Elder

It is said that marigolds, particularly the Mexican variety *tagetes minuta*, will control these weeds. It may be disconcerting to the visitor to see a dense crop of marigolds blazing in some unsuitable part of the garden, but if this remedy works as effectively as turnips against couch who cares?

Give them excess of it

The growth of perennial weeds, particularly of a fleshy kind, can be discouraged by allowing them to grow happily till just about to flower and then harvesting them and laying them back again thickly on the surface over the roots. If you have two areas infested, lay all that you have cut on one area first, and the treatment there is the more likely to be effective. You can even search out patches of the same weed in waste ground and harvest that for the purpose.

CONTROLLING DISEASES

Hang Mothballs on your Peach tree

We carefully sprayed our peach against leaf curl, and still the leaves curled. 'Pick off the affected leaves,' said an Old Wife, 'and hang a few moth-balls about on the tree.' No more leaf curl that year, though until then we seemed to be spend-ing most of our time picking off affected leaves

and spraying with this and that. Finding ordinary mothballs at one time hard to get we tried Mothax rings; they proved equally effective and much easier to hang. To guard against a reputation for eccentricity, the reason for decorating a peach like a Christmas tree with white balls or pretty mauve rings should be explained to visitors.

Meths

Any methylated spirits that can be spared should be used to spray sprouts and cabbages against mildew.

Clubroot

Bury a stick of rhubarb here and there in the bed when planting cabbages, against clubroot.

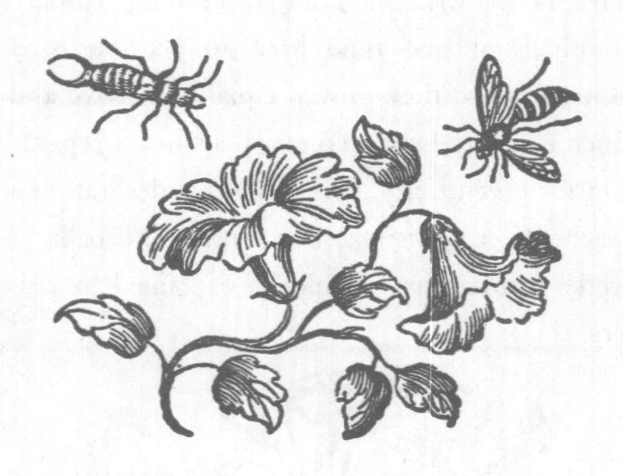

PESTS

Step on it

A member of the panel of the BBC's admirable Gardeners' Question Time programme, speaking of identifying small creatures in the garden, said that as a lad he was told: 'If it moves slowly enough, step on it; if it doesn't, leave it—it'll probably kill something else.'

Never spray against Greenfly

There is a giant conspiracy between the insecticide manufacturers and writers on gardening to encourage the public to spend fortunes and waste hours spraying their roses against aphids.

A single clove of garlic planted beside each rose is guaranteed by the present writers (who have not been bought by the lobby—though perhaps only because they have never been approached) absolutely to keep greenfly from the plant. The roots will take up from the soil a substance from the garlic inimical to greenfly, and if in early spring a few hatch out from eggs of parents careless of their offspring's welfare they will neither lay nor survive themselves. Whatever it is that the rose takes up from the garlic does not affect its own scent, and so long as the garlic is not allowed to flower there will be no odour of garlic in the garden. Try it for one year with one group of roses in one bed protected only by garlic, spraying all the others in the garden as much as you need, and you will never waste money or time again. All members of the onion family, including chives, are partially effective, but garlic is the only completely efficient answer, the systemic insecticide to end all others. In very dry weather, water the garlic so that the excretions from its roots will be sure to be taken up by the thirsty rose.

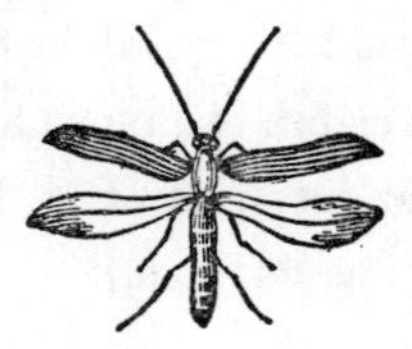

Woolly Aphis and Whitefly

Nasturtiums are said to be your answer to aphids on fruit trees, growing the long trailing kind wound up the trunks; and also against whitefly in the greenhouse. If the latter is true it must be because of exhalation rather than of emanation from the roots, since most greenhouse plants are grown in pots and the Old Wives do not suggest growing a nasturtium in every one.

Ants

Our ancestors were more anti-ant than we are, blaming them for much of the damage done by aphids. 'If,' writes an old herbalist, 'you stamp lupins (which are to be had at the Apothecaries) and therewith rub round the bottom or lower part of any tree, no ants or pismires will go up and touch the same tree.' [I started to look up 'pismire' in the dictionary, to provide a scholarly footnote, but decided that I would sooner retain my own fantasy image of a fabulous monster like those in a mediaeval bestiary, all the more terrible for being only an eighth of an inch long. Then, a sense of academic duty prevailing, I did look it up; and all it said was 'ant'. B.B.]

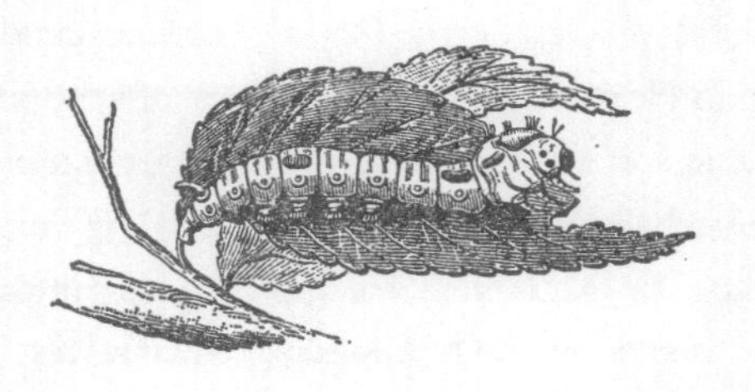

Caterpillars

Robert Ball, a Member of the Royal Society, wrote at length to the gardener Richard Bradley in 1718 about how all noxious pests, notably caterpillars, were borne in great clouds on the east wind, originating in Tartary. Windbreaks of trees, high hedges and wattle fences should therefore be placed to protect the whole garden or particular plants from that side, for no caterpillars would be found to the west of them.

Earwigs

The same Mr Bradley advised hanging 'Hoggs-hoofs, the Bowls of Tobacco-Pipes and Lobster-claws on the tops of sticks' among plants 'and killing the vermin that lodge in them every morning'.

Slugs

Richard Bradley 'learned from a curious gentleman in Hertfordshire' of the efficacy of wrapping the trunk of a fruit tree with two or three strands of horsehair 'so full of stubs and straggling Points of the Hair that neither a slug nor a snail can pass over them without wounding themselves to Death'. For wall-grown trees he recommended nailing the horsehair rope to the wall completely outlining the tree; for espaliers, winding one strand round the bottom of the stem and one round the bottom of each stake. For cauliflowers a rope should be laid all round the bed.

A shortage of horsehair ropes in this degenerate age need not induce despair: an admirable trap may be made with a little beer in a jam jar laid on its side.

FAUNA AMONG THE FLORA

Deer

In a woodland district, the only sure way to keep deer out of a garden is to build a wall nine feet high all round it, or a solid wooden paling whose

upkeep would cost more in the long run than the outlay on a wall. The rugosa rose Alba will grow to seven feet high and make in time a dense, impenetrable hedge; but if deer can jump nine feet high what is their long jump record? One remembers the stag in *The Lady of the Lake*: 'With one brave bound the copse he cleared'. Anyway, rugosas will not grow well under trees, and our garden in places blends into the surrounding woods; to erect a paling in these sections would be a sin. After we had lived here a short while we realised that we could never sacrifice the sight of the deer, at sunrise and at dusk, passing through the garden and pausing to drink at stream or pond; but all the young shoots of our roses were nibbled off. We planted enormous tree-climbing varieties like Himalayan musk and Kiftsgate which will grow to thirty or forty feet, and protected their lower stems with chicken wire while they were young, and such huge shrub roses as Nevada, whose lower outside shoots alone suffered. We read that sprinkling lion manure would terrify the deer, and could well believe it; but then keeping the lions to provide the manure would terrify us (though we also read that lion skins would make another useful by-product, for wrapping clothes in them would infallibly keep out moths).

Then an Old Wife provided a much easier solution. Tie an old piece of thick cloth such as flannel on the end of a bamboo cane and dunk it in creosote, and stick it in the ground like a little flag near each rose, or at each corner of a bed. The deer will not risk coming near the strong smell, which will prevent them scenting the approach of danger. After a day or so the smell will not be apparent to humans unless they actually sniff the cloth. The flags should be re-dipped at intervals during the summer if there is heavy rain. The scent of violets will (in humans, too) have the effect of temporarily paralysing the olfactory nerve after a few moments, but their flowering season is not long enough to serve instead of creosote to protect your roses.

Birds

Alarmed at the expense of wire netting for our fruit cage, we used nylon netting. The squirrels sat on the crossbars gnawing neat holes, through which so many birds entered that we soon seemed to be keeping an aviary rather than a fruit cage.

We reverted to the Old Wives' practice of winding threads of black cotton about among the fruit; the birds have difficulty judging the distance of such threads against the sky and fear entangling their wings if they have to take off in a hurry. It is, at any rate, a deterrent. Nylon thread will not snap when branches are blown about in the wind, or when (undeterred) birds do blunder into it.

One Old Wife has proved that primulas and yellow crocus, elsewhere ruined by birds, are left untouched growing beside a lavender hedge. We propose to grow lavender among our soft fruit, at any rate along the back of a strawberry bed; it will do no harm to try it, but we shall watch the growth and flavour of the berries compared with others grown elsewhere, for strawberries are kittle cattle and may dislike the proximity of so strong a herb.

Moles

Small lumps of acetylene fuel put down the runs are effective, the damp in the soil activating them; but they should be stored in a really air-tight container. We had kept some in a damp shed in a too loosely-covered jar; it was greyish instead of black when we used it, and we found a new hill the next day in the place where we had just removed the old one, with the fuel, now white, cheerfully crumbled among the freshly turned earth of the new run.

Gerard, the sixteenth-century herbalist, advises the placing of garlic in the mouth of a mole's run, 'and you shall see him run out, astonied'.

We did, and we waited, and we didn't. Perhaps we did not wait long enough.

The growing of caper spurge in the garden is also recommended as a deterrent; we grow caper spurge, and it may deter some, but living on the edge of woodland we have so many moles that unless the whole garden was full of nothing but caper spurge it is unlikely that it would deter them all.

But if molehills you have, use the beautifully crumbled soil, mixed with sand, for potting.

Cats

An Old Wife, troubled with neighbours' cats that rolled on her catmint and lay sunning themselves on her favourite alpines, wrote to a national newspaper that she had discovered a cure: lay a length of the inner tube of a bicycle tyre on the lawn, and the cats will think it a snake and give the garden a wide berth.

Wild Cats

If you are troubled with these, it is said that they 'will flee from the smoke of rue and bitter almonds'.

Flower-Arrangers

'Shee that would have posies is a sore tryall to the good Husbandman of his Garden,' as some old herbalist might well have said, except that the vice of flower-arranging is a comparatively modern one. Admittedly much of the space in old gardens must have been taken up with the growing of 'strewing herbs' for mixing with the straw that preceded carpets, both for sweet scents and for aromas that deterred mice, fleas and lice. But it was the Dutch flower-painters who (largely, we suspect, to encourage the sale of Dutch bulbs in the 'tulipomania' period) popularised the notion of massing mixed flowers in vases. The Japanese, who create masterpieces with three twigs, must be far less unpopular with their gardeners. The flower-arranger who is not a gardener should never be let loose with a knife or scissors out of doors, particularly near shrubs. Since mantraps are now illegal, the best way to ensure that anything is left flowering in the garden at all is to see to it that such flowers as are brought into the house last long there before they need replacing.

All flowers will last longer in water if foxgloves are incorporated in the arrangement. If their presence is not considered suitable for a particular artistic effect, add foxglove tea to the water: pour boiling water on a handful of leaves and flowers, or leaves alone if the flowers are not in season, and allow them to steep overnight. Put pennies in the water. For delphiniums and larkspur, add sugar; for daffodils and narcissi, add charcoal or camphor. Put the cut ends of chrysanthemums in very hot water for a moment and then straight into very cold. Wrap the stalks of tulips as soon as they are cut in newspaper and stand them for several hours up to their necks in water. Daffodils (which excrete a substance poisonous to other flowers and the handling of whose stems even gives some people a rash) should preferably not be mixed with anything else in a vase, but if the arranger insists see that they are soaked first for an hour in separate water and then rinsed again. Topmost buds should be nipped from delphiniums, gladioli and snap-dragons.

Heathers will last for weeks in the house without the flowers withering or the needles dropping off if they are kept without water—a fact which is particularly useful with the winter and early spring flowering varieties. Forsythia and winter-sweet will last longer if picked in bud and stood first in hot water than if picked already in flower. If flowering shrubs must be used, not just the flowering tips should be cut but the whole of the flowering shoot down to two buds above the old wood.

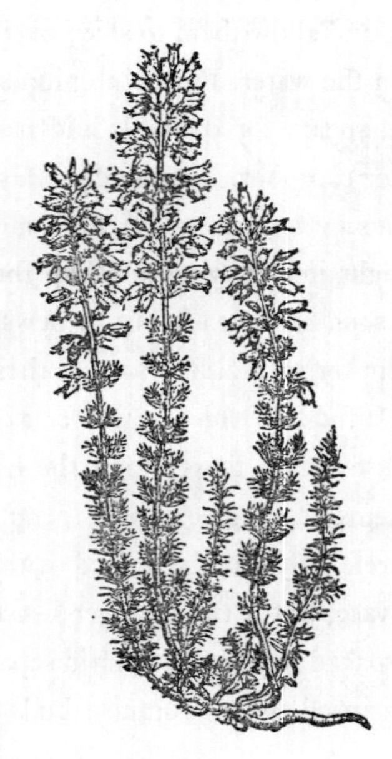

WASTE NOT

Kitchen refuse

Anything you can eat plants can use too. Even caviar could no doubt be added to fishmeal with good effect. The outer leaves of vegetables need not even be composted but can be used as green manure, either chopped up fine and dug into the lower spit of soil when planting or into the top spit several months before any planting is to be done there. The contents of the sink basket should go on the compost heap, with the caveat that meat scraped from plates should be excluded: foxes, and even some dogs, will scatter the whole heap about if they smell it. One peculiarity that we cannot explain is that, although coffee grounds scattered on the heap in the ordinary way seemed of no interest to animals, grounds thrown there in the little paper cones used in Melitta coffee filters were always carefully extracted and the paper, cleaned out, scattered far and wide. We blamed the foxes on general principle. We had the impression that they said to each other: 'Let's go up to the farm for a chicken dinner and then down to the Bolands for coffee,' but a zoologist tells us we imagined the whole thing.

Tea-leaves

Old Wives, when they have finished telling fortunes, save their tea-leaves to put as a mulch on camellias, which benefit particularly from them.

Milk

When milk bottles are to be rinsed they should first be filled with water and well shaken, and the contents used as a very mild liquid manure on houseplants and in the garden. Climbers planted against house walls always tend to get too dry. and luckily for the housewife she need not go far from the kitchen to find a useful place to rinse out her bottles.

Soapy water

Before the days of detergents, Old Wives recommended the throwing away of soapy water, particularly if it had soda in it, on flower and vegetable beds, saying that cabbages benefited particularly. People who, like us, have septic tanks and should not use detergents can at least be grateful for this by-product of their labours.

Banana skins

Laid just below the surface of the soil, banana skins have long been said to be very good for roses, and scientists now approve the practice, having found that they are able to provide, as they rot quickly, a considerable quantity of calcium, magnesium, sulphur, phosphates, sodium and silica.

Beer

Charlie, whom we meet on our country bus when we go shopping, tells us that he once threw what was left after brewing home-made beer out of his kitchen window. There was a row of holly-hocks just outside, and, while the rest of the row did reasonably well, the hollyhock immediately below the window grew to a height of eighteen foot six inches, 'and a man from the BBC came down to see it'. Rinse out your beer bottles and glasses, like your milk bottles, for the good of the garden. It is in this case, apparently, the yeast that does the trick.

Boots

Never throw old boots and shoes in the dustbin, but bury them in the garden. Leather is full of good things, and they will rot down eventually, except for loathsome rubber and plastic soles which can then be retrieved. The salts in human sweat are not without their uses, either.

Egg boxes

Do not give your egg boxes back to the grocer or milkman, far less throw them away: they are just as good for growing small seedlings as peat pots, and cost you nothing.

Old Nylons

Nylon stockings are strong enough and have enough give in them to make perfect tree ties.

A Use for Horsetail

Gerard says that horsetail was known also as pewterwort, and that it was used for scouring pewter dishes and wooden implements in the kitchen. It can also be used for cleaning aluminium if you run out of wirewool. Make a little stubby two-ended brush about three inches long by binding a bunch of the stems with two pieces of string about half an inch apart. Both the sides and ends of this can be used. If, as is to be hoped, you have eliminated it from the garden, look for it growing wild in damp places. If an aluminium saucepan has been burnt, first boil an onion in it and pour off the scum that will rise.

WEATHER

In these days of weather-forecasting satellites, old methods may be despised; but meteorological offices only give us a very broad general picture, and old people in the district should always be listened to for ways of foretelling local conditions. On our summer holidays in France as children we always knew that it was going to rain next day if we could see distinctly the white cliffs of the Kentish coast across that narrowest reach of the Channel; and from a certain flat in Rome the same could be said if you could pick out actual houses on the distant slopes of the Alban hills.

In *The Country Calendar or the Shepherd of Banbury's Rules*, of the late seventeenth century, there is a pleasing variant, given in three languages, of the old adage 'Red sky at night, Shepherd's delight, Red in the morning, Shepherd's warning'. It gives us a pleasing picture of the pilgrim trudging across Europe in older times: 'In England,' writes the author, John Claridge,

A red evening and a grey morning
Sets the Pilgrim a Walking.

In *French* thus:

Le rouge Soir, & blanc Matin,
Font rejouir le Pèlerin.

The *Italians* say the same:

Sera rosa, & nigro Matino,
Allegro il Peregrino.

He also quotes an English proverb:

In the Decay of the Moon,
A cloudy Morning bodes a fair Afternoon.

Again:

When Clouds appear like Rocks and Towers,
The Earth's refreshed by frequent Showers.

He says that his own observation has confirmed the saying that a general mist before sunrise near the full moon denotes fair weather for a fortnight; if this is seen in the new moon, there will be wet weather in the last fortnight as it grows old; but he warns us not to predict from the first night of the new moon but from a couple of nights later.

In hot weather, when the wind has been southerly for two or three days, he says, and clouds are piled like towers one on another with black on the nether side, there will be thunder and rain suddenly; and if two such castles arise one on either hand, it is time to take shelter hastily. If clouds 'look dusky, or of a tarnish silver colour, and move very slowly, it is a Sign of Hail, which if there be a Mixture of Blue in the Clouds will be small, but if very yellow, large.' Above all things, he advises us, watch the bees, for if it is going to rain they will not leave the hives, or fly only short distances from them.

We make no apology for quoting proverbs, for, as Bacon said, 'they are the philosophy of the common people'. Here is a versified collection of many of them from *The New Book of Knowledge*, published in 1758:

If ducks and drakes their wings do flutter high,
Or tender colts upon their backs do lie;
If sheep do bleat or play and skip about,
Or swine hide by straw bearing on their snout;
If oxen lick themselves against the hair,
Or grazing kine to feed apace appear;
If cattle bellow, gazing from below,
Or if dogs' entrails rumble to and fro;
If doves and pigeons in the evening come

Later than usual to their dovehouse home;
If crows and daws do oft themselves bewet,
Or ants and pismires home apace do get;
If in the dust hens do their pinions shake,
Or by their flocking a great number make;
If swallows fly upon the water low,
Or woodlice seem in armies for to go;
If flies or gnats or fleas infest and bite,
Or sting more than their wont by day and night;
If toads hie home or frogs do croak amain,
Or peacocks cry—soon after look for rain.

Mouffet, in the seventeenth-century *Theatre of Insects*, observes that 'if gnats at sunset do play up and down in open air, they presage heat; but if they altogether sting those that pass by, then cold weather and much rain'. They will help you, he says, to find water in times of drought, where, after sunrise, 'they whirl round in an obelisk'.

Dry weather

However foretold, when the dry weather comes we must water. Sages advise us to water only in the mornings between mid-September and May; even when watering-in new plants, it should not be done late in the day lest, icy at night, it damage the roots.

We read that when planting a peach you should sink a pipe an inch and half or more in diameter and a couple of feet long upright alongside it, with its top just above the surface, and water into this in hot weather, to encourage the roots to go down and to supply them with enough moisture there. As we grow several huge roses such as Kiftsgate and Himalayan musk up trees we set such pipes down alongside them, for they have to be planted close to the trunks of the trees where the soil tends to be always dry. Although properly speaking, of course, water from a butt should always be used, this is a slow process if one has to stand by the quickly-filling and slowly-emptying pipe with a can; so in a long dry season, we confess, we turn on the hose, put the end down the pipe, and leave it slowly trickling for as much as a quarter of an hour; and, at any rate, on a steep sandy hillside we have roses growing thirty feet high after five years, doing well, and bidding fair to grow another ten feet or so.

The gardener of a palazzo in Rome, responsible for the staggering display of plants in the great earthenware containers on the terraces,

amazed us by saying that he only watered them twice a week even in the height of summer. Each container had two or three holes at the bottom of the front surface; these would be stopped with bungs, and the container watered till two inches of water stood on the surface of the soil for a quarter of an hour; then the bungs would be taken out. Any tendency for the soil to leach out was combated by frequent top dressing with mulches, and the removal of some of the soil every autumn and digging in quantities of manure—usually a mixture of sheep dung and a leaf-and-bark compost. Certainly huge azaleas and oleanders flourished under this treatment as well as geraniums, plumbago, and such; but even fuchsias did not suffer from it.

Cold weather

When frost is expected, plants in need of protection should, to our surprise, be sprayed with cold water in the evening, which will generate enough heat in evaporating to prevent frost damage.

After a hot, dry summer, the bracken, so useful to cover plants with against frost, tends to have very little substance and after a few weeks to have shrivelled almost away. At such times the top-hamper of Michaelmas daises can be cut back as soon as flowering is over and used for the same purpose; piled cross-hatched it will give almost as good cover, and is practically indestructible, as anyone will know who has been foolish enough to include it in the compost heap.

Would that we knew why
and where and in what weather
was the anonymous poet when he wrote:
O western wind, when wilt thou blow,
That the small rain down shall rain
Christ, that my love were in my arms,
And I in my bed again!

INDEX